SUBTERRANEA

Jos Smith
SUBTERRANEA

2016

Published by Arc Publications
Nanholme Mill, Shaw Wood Road,
Todmorden OL14 6DA, UK
www.arcpublications.co.uk

Copyright © Jos Smith, 2016
Copyright in the present edition © Arc Publications, 2016
Design by Tony Ward
Printed by TJ International, Padstow, Cornwall

978 1910345 70 2 (pbk)
978 1910345 71 9 (hbk)
978 1910345 72 6 (ebk)

Acknowledgements

Some of these poems, or earlier versions of them, have appeared in the following magazines: *The Clearing, Conversation Papers, The Island Review, Magma, Poetry Wales* and *The Rialto*. 'Stugged' won 3rd place in the Richard Jefferies Poetry Competition 2013 and 'Witness' was published in the anthology *Entanglements* (Two Ravens Press, 2012). The sequence 'A Plume of Smoke' was originally published as a pamphlet by Maquette Press in 2015. These latter poems owe a debt to Dr. Timothy Cooper and Dr Anna Green's British Academy funded research project concerning the Torrey Canyon oil spill.

Cover image
by Mark Edmonds.

This book is in copyright. Subject to statutory exception and to provision of relevant collective licensing agreements, no reproduction of any part of this book may take place without the written permission of Arc Publications.

Editor for the UK and Ireland:
John W. Clarke

for Bianca

CONTENTS

Leaving / 11
Cothelstone / 12
The Edge of Magic / 13
Stugged / 14
A Whole Herd of Bodies with Round Lashed Eyes / 16
Scapula / 17
Witness / 18
from A Plume of Smoke
  Herbivore / 19
  Fiat / 20
  The Smell was the First Thing / 21
  Unspeakables / 22
  Solution / 23
  Birds / 24
  Quarry at Chouet Headland, Guernsey / 25
  Beacon / 26
  Miniatures / 27
  Afterwards / 28
Landscape Interrupted / 30
Berries / 32
Landscape with Crows / 33
Pitching Under Hay Bluff / 34
Storm / 35
Grimpen / 36
Tiresias at the Galway Institute for Environment, Marine and Energy / 37
The Heat / 38
Years Later / 39
A Parish Map / 40
Skew / 42
Harbledown Solstice / 43
Home Ground / 44
Muffled / 45

Thaw / 46
Slow Landscapes
　I Near Twyford / 47
　II Cubbington / 48
　III Ruins, Stoke Mandeville / 49
The Cliff Railway / 50
Hawthorn / 51
Blocks / 52
Ultima Thule / 54
Annunciation / 55

Biographical Note / 57

*'There are more places within a forest,
among the galaxies or on a Connemara seashore,
than the geometry of common sense allows.'*

Tim Robinson

LEAVING

I am thinking of you as I stoop to pick them up
two long willow leaves, dried together,
our last night alone in the empty house
coiled up rust-red from tip to stem,
your tanned back fitting the length of me,
both emptied of the living sap,
shadows of the summer we lived here
resigned to the ebb of their season's lot
as memory begins its affectionate work
in one final chapter of fragile form, held,
our night together on the palm of my hand,
a stripped bed blown with autumn willow leaves.

COTHELSTONE

The hill is a big round dream of various slopes,
rising and leaning, pledging and dropping away.
Beneath the hill
        another hill,
        an inner hill,
        a bigger one
shouts up through its own dark earth
to the sky's upturned deafness.

Swelling with rains and shrinking in heat,
flashing with light through silent clouds,
raising two beech clumps, a ruined tower,
paths, ponies, walkers, solstice dancers
and who knows how many graves.

A hill like a planet adrift,
watching the valley of Taunton Dean,
clenched in tree roots and gushing with leaves
carrying the living and the dead on its back.

THE EDGE OF MAGIC

Miranda walks to the west of the island,
to the storm beach knee-deep in plastic debris,

sun-bleached and weather-battered tupperware,
frayed lengths of rope and polystyrene shapes

(packing, she thinks, for fish, or electrical goods).
She crouches as if it were a bed of flowers.

A burst blue football today, a wetsuit shoe,
a pale, pink bottle the shape of a woman's body.

This is her secret. Low tide, the kissing waves.
Two cuckoos chuckle as they chase inland.

It's hard to tell what strings have been pulled
for her good life here on the island. She is starting

to distrust the weather, for example. Or flowers
like the purple-mouthed balsam by the streams,

the acres of tunnel in the rhododendrons
she played in as a child. All of them

under some loose enchantment, a father's magic
in its twilight years, fraying at the island edges.

STUGGED

> *Dartmoor: richer in its bowels than in its face thereof*
> TRISTRAM RISDON

Falling asleep in a horseshoe turf-tie
under a wind-flat khaki bivouac,
all the soldier can think about
is the give of moss underfoot as if he's falling.

It lives in the body like an echo:
that crunch and the weight of him
dropping through the step.
He thinks of the joke
about a man they found in the mire
by his hat, of his view
through the peat-black dreamscape below,
its half swallowed hawthorns and their
bright, strangled roots, its boulders
like teeth gone astray through the flesh.
A dream of shotguns overhead, blasts
given down through the legs of a man,
the unthinkable speed of lead
crying out through the sky.
A dream of the rhythm
of shoed hooves thumping,
of muffled voices and the sudden,
sharp noise of dogs baying at a burrow.

Soon deep silence
like an aura packed in the dark.
The mudded skeleton of a cow curled up,
afloat in a congealed night sky
like an idea laid to rest in the back of the mind.
Bangles and brooches and knotted gold
glinting, lost in the prickling flesh
of long-decayed heather like stars in the pools
that remember what we were never here to see.

And the soldier is sleeping now, with the cow
and the drowned noise of the dogs
still ringing in the mouth of the burrow,
fast asleep in the mind of the moor with the man
who is not there, who has gone down now,
off through the dark below his hat.

A WHOLE HERD OF BODIES WITH ROUND LASHED EYES

Imagine a poem for the Friesians on Cadbury Hill.
A giant, nervous poem with a growling belly
that stands uneasily upright on the page, waiting
for the reader to move along, move along, go.

A poem that carries its vowels in canvas stretchers,
staggering perhaps, grave and over-emotional,
full of hormones not all its own; easily startled.
A cow like these would appreciate a soft poem.

Wide stanzas that lean on one another
and breathe back and forth with cavernous lungs
and wonder about the shape of the moon at night.
The moon who always knows what a cow is thinking.

A poem that begins the way only the meek can lead
but drags behind it the whole of human language
clattering like pots and pans in the swimming mist. Cow-curiosity,
muscling forward when the reader's back is turned.

A slow and searching inquiry, like a whole herd of bodies
with round, lashed eyes, expectantly waiting
for the answer to a question that you might have missed,
that perhaps even they have misheard.

Imagine a poem for the Friesians on Cadbury Hill.
A poem that offers its wet nose up,
muddling its soul through bloodshot eyes,
balancing passions mysterious, even to itself.

SCAPULA

> Two poems originally written onto either side of the scapula of a cow found near Erme Head on Dartmoor and returned to the same place.

Gusts

An uphill stampede of nothing over the grass.
Nothing feeling its way through the foliage of the air,
all hands and hair and somersaulting weight,
chasing out a space between the earth and sky.
One pulls long strokes close to the ground;
one lurches, twists and buries its head in
smithereens of light; one shoulders the underside
of ravens courting; each one faceless and rowdy,
throwing sunshine ahead of itself and charging
through the doors of the sky, eyes closed. Until
they vanish. Collected, from nowhere, into a sudden

Lull

Now the flowers ease out their broadest show of colour yet
as if there had never been such a thing as the wind.
Were there anything more they could do to share the sun's
rich heat but follow its arc fastidiously, they would do it.
Air stares down on itself from a still point in the sky.
For a moment, it is able to rest on the earth at its feet.
Strange place, this grass-grown hill of peat,
this granite clitter scattered with horse dung.
The air leans too far, forgets itself. Towering
there, it comes unpoised. Falls at a startling
rate of speed, and is shredded into Gusts

WITNESS

A latter-day Noah might have set up camp here,
drunk his wine from a pigskin clenched in a fist,
bitten his lip and drowned that inextinguishable grief.
Here where the Black Ridge slopes to the south
and Hangingstone Hill to the north, a plateau so high
you can see the fog kneel down and deliver
the Okement, the Dart, the Taw, the Teign and the Tavy.

And remember, when the waters were high in the world
the ocean made an island of this moor. And remember,
when the glaciers came down from the north,
dragging their bite across the Earth, they stopped
short of these heights, and shuffled off their moraine.

To these few miles of upland heath, of blanket bog
and valleys draining out toward the sea, is left
the pristine quiet of survival, air with its ears ringing.
As with the prophet whose lot is to live and remember,
an aureole borne so high, pronged with its unscathed
tors, weighs heavy. In such stone, gravity's closed
eyes; in such stone, silence kept between the teeth.

A PLUME OF SMOKE[1]

> *When we go down to the low-tide line, we enter a world that is as old as the earth itself – the primeval meeting place of the elements of earth and water, a place of compromise and conflict and eternal change.*
> RACHEL CARSON, *The Edge of the Sea*

HERBIVORE

This westerly coast is one long animal
laid down in the slopes of cove and cliff,
bristling with sea life like nerves in the skin:

the swollen pores of purple anemones,
rolling tongues of whelks in their shells,
the half-formed thoughts of blue fire jellyfish,

all a part of the one lounging body,
easing back and forth in a shallow niche
where Atlantic groans open into hissing foam.

It touches the currents with whiskered prawns,
it listens in clouds of sand on the seabed,
moves as warmth in a forest of algae.

An animal, drifting in and out of view,
breathing and sleeping, sniffing and eating,
grazing the outer edge of a volatile world.

---

[1] In March 1967 the Torrey Canyon ran aground on rocks off the coast of Cornwall spilling over one hundred thousand tonnes of crude oil into the sea. It was the first major incident of a kind that has become all too familiar over subsequent decades.

Fiat

We dreamed of black reservoirs,
secretions beneath the desert sand,
sea life pressed and melted down
to hydrophobic ooze; foraminifera
forgotten into strata of the earth.

Let that which goes down rise up,
let that which sinks to the floor of the sea
brighten with fire; ignite in chambers,
swell the empty air with buried heat.

So it comes, lured up, piped out,
cracked open into fractions, refined,
arriving from all directions over the seas;
at night, almost sullen, poured ashore
and brought to us, asleep, where we dream.

The Smell was the First Thing

Mary Glassbrook stood on her lawn
at dawn, red sun up behind the pines,
– almost unable to breathe.

Edward Berry threw open the windows
cursing his brand new heating system
– but the worst of it flooded in.

You ate it you drank it you slept in it
when you woke up it was right there
staring you down every morning for days.

The weight leaned in and belittled you.
Every part of it found you out
with hands spread wide.

This is how events arrive:
intimate long before
any kind of explanation.

You'll find your way through the thicket of air;
there'll be others in the street there waiting;
you'll wrestle with superstitions.

You'll do it together thank god,
but it won't slow the fear, the realisation
that something is different this time.

Unspeakables

It came to rest in Holywell Bay,
six to nine inches deep at the half-tide mark.
If you dropped a stone through
to the water below a hole remained,
staring back up with nothing to say.
Solidified lumps rolled up the beach.

A sense of failure came in on that tide,
eight miles by nightfall, twenty by morning,
folding softly on the rocks below us
and hanging over the bay like a plague.
Or rather, an arch and technical diagnosis
that none of us understood.

For when you just can't get the problem,
for when you can't find the words to address it,
for when matters at arm's-length repeatedly
confound – there's news like this
of an offshore event.
Silence and a plume of smoke.

Solution

Turning off the motor and drifting
while the brothers worked the pump in oilskins
hosing barrels of detergent overboard,
for a moment, we could have been in another world.

Thick mist with chemical rainbows warping about us
and the black rind on the water still as leather.
Like a life-sized model Atlantic: placid, ethereal,
Arthurian film set; or derelict warehouse,
the wild ocean somehow vanished underneath.

The skin came off our fingertips
and a burning in the eyes; inflammation
of the lungs, acute pharyngitis, we were told.

Fighting a vile pollutant with another
that sounded so homely: 'detergent'.
It worked though. It broke up the oil
so all the surrounding sea life could swallow it whole.

Birds

I remember a boy with a satchel collecting cormorants
one by one and bringing them home on the bus.

The bus driver asking "What's in the satchel?"
and letting him ride for free for the rest of the day.

I remember a hair salon given to cleaning razorbills:
wild eyed, black beaks closed with elastic bands.

And how many bathtubs in how many homes
were stained with oil from feathers over the coming days?

Shopping bags of mackerel run between cottages.
The swapping of soaps and tips from those who knew.

While the army drove their barrels back and forth
you did what you could but it didn't really help.

I remember three children stood on a beach
calling out "Don't land! Don't land! Don't land!"

Quarry at Chouet Headland, Guernsey

The way a tumour gets its hooks into the gut,
thousands of tons were pumped into a coastal quarry.

A landscape like an ongoing dream
dreamed out in the open with lasting effect.

The palpable sump of a long-held urge to hide
displaced into sickness arrived by sea;

the force that through the black ooze drove
drives not down here, a stone's throw from the breakers.

Now every time they syphon it off
more bubbles up from the sediment below.

A memory that we have been ill equipped to meet
with anything but the same helplessness

for over forty years. Little corner of disaster
kept warm for another generation to work.

Huge dark magnet to circumspect birds,
breather of tall fumes under the summer sun,

sleeping digester of unliftable wings,
you have been on the coastal edge of all of our thoughts.

BEACON

From the roaring Sea Vixen,
several thousand pound bombs
toppled and turned through the air.

From the Hunters,
'drop tanks', pillars of white water,
and napalm in curtains of flame.

The third Buccaneer assault
hit the mark with all the signs
of a nuclear explosion.

A fireball rose rapidly on a thin black stem,
teetering up through a westerly Force 1
and mushroomed at three thousand feet.

The wreck fell apart, burned, poured out
a flaming slick that spread down tide. Primal,
like land forming where there was no land.

Smoke-pluming Quokelunde, Forest of Scilly risen,
Black Lyonnesse 'which the low tide discovereth,'
token of the wasted ground opened before us.

Through the afternoon and into the evening
families climbed the hills east of Sennen Cove.
One stood in anoraks on the crest of Carn Brea.

Carn Brea: that barrow, summit cairn,
hermitage and chapel; that Radar station
and beacon; first hill and last hill in England

where many have buried their dead
near the edge of the world,
bristling with nerves about what comes after this.

Miniatures

1.

Sunshine on the water like hot coals.
A raven slips over the cliff edge,
balancing the sky on her back;
drops it, catches it; winks and caws.

2.

Flower heads of sea pink
prickled up from nothing on the rocks,
holding their little breaths in a fistful of soil.
This, when all hell glares inland from the Atlantic.

3.

The hawthorn has been empty for months
but, this morning, opens foam-white with flowers
as if the spirit of the bush, mid-way through
abandoning the soil, were reassured by the sun.

Afterwards

The wet head of something will rise from the pools,
dripping and lonely and not what it was.

Animals will regard it with suspicion.
It may even despise itself for a while.

But whatever comes
comes faithful to the day:

the algae in disturbing profusion,
as if the sea itself were full and spilling over;

the green weed grown over every stationary rock,
heaven-shuddering green with nothing left to eat it;

and birdless silence,
leaning in over the land from the sky.

Clean, intelligent silence
already stirring the fish below it.

Enduring, kind silence
like a thirst that knows where it's going,

like a promise being kept against all odds,
consoling nothing.

LANDSCAPE INTERRUPTED

The deer has come no one doubts
from the treeline that ionizing radiations
to the edge of the meadow increase mutation rates.

She is overwhelmed that most mutation rates
by the deep orange space of it are deleterious.
The rosehips in the hedge and that some damage
begin to glow to human life and to ecological systems.

She can hardly bare it is therefore likely to result
it takes five minutes from the increase in radiation levels
to come as far as the purple clover flowers.

Perhaps it is the warmth she has come for
small as it might be the lift the early light works
that will inevitably be caused by the operation
in the dew of large numbers of power plants.

Two squirrels chase up an oak tree
but while all scientists agree on these facts,
and she nearly bolts, individually they differ
– but the flowers are good as to the levels
of radiation they consider tolerable.

And as the sun rises because this involves social considerations
she feels that warmth in her fur based on value judgements
pores flowering open in a wave along her spine.

Head up. She blinks, licks her nose.
The biological hazards it is too much
resulting from the industrial use of nuclear power
she treads between the brambles must be balanced against
    the advantages

ducks back into the dark to be derived
from the economic development and is gone.

BERRIES

We were looking for your best side,
a single photograph that captured HAWTHORN
an image that said CLIFFTOP ENDURANCE
or showed on a calm blue day
the loose direction of a decade's wind.

What we found were these berries
the colour of dried blood
– *here take them, have them, they are yours, anyone's* –
while the spirit of the tree passed out below,
sifting back down through the earth.

Whose black skeleton is this left here then?
Whose troubled silhouette,
home from home for Sweeney working his claws?
Who will remember these blackening berries
as the blind Atlantic wind swallows them whole?

LANDSCAPE WITH CROWS

Crows – that remind me of a broken window.
Or a damp, soot-coloured firework.
Crows that scatter, manhandle the air as they climb.
Crows that frame this and that as they go
like those Friesians wading downhill.
Crows that build a world with a cry:
"Each each each to his own."

The land is an oblique plane underneath.
I have many polite questions.
I have hurried here and am ready now,
but the stillness glares back.
Don't ask questions. Listen.
Intelligence radiates permanently upwards.
Start with nothing. Wait. Crows in the sky.
Start with crows. Crows, as if for the first time.

PITCHING UNDER HAY BLUFF

> *The coarser pleasures of my boyish days,*
> *And their glad animal movements*
>   WORDSWORTH

Four miles to go at the end of the day is
a long way to drag our blistered feet
over pocked and puddled upland heath
in an ice-flecked wind...

Four miles to go at the end of the day is
a ragged noise of inhale, exhale,
toe-stub rhythms in the glazed and helpless
weight of the head...

Four miles to go at the end of the day is a ludicrous,
knackered euphoria that can't believe
and can't believe and seems to have
come apart in the middle...

Four miles and three miles till the bluff drops north
on a meadow lit with yellow flowers,
and we dump our packs and feel that swell
like a breaking out of wings.

And the yellow flowers are closing their heads
and the sun is gone and the day is done, we hit
the ground and fall asleep as if the ground
were water.

Breaths held now,
we stare below us
at flowers withdrawing
like fireflies into the earth.

STORM

Before the storm that will not materialise
as a storm, but a slow, clean fog droved in
by some great weight of Atlantic air,
Grimspound looks never more abandoned
from the stones of Hookney Tor.

Nearly three thousand years old:
a settled ruin on the saddle between hills,
leaning toward the West Weburn.
                    About now
they might have been gathering in livestock,
mothers calling to children. Wolves, maybe
even a bear or two out tonight.

Shunting the timber over the gate,
I see him look up. He catches my eye,
pauses for a moment and sniffs, as if something
were not quite right with the weather.

GRIMPEN

> *On the edge of a grimpen, where is no secure foothold*
> T. S. Eliot

Wasteland, prison, and crime scene are the shadows
cast by 'grim' in 'grimpen'; half tremendous mire,
half the treachery of a criminal mind, that shows
its ugly noumena balancing deceit in superstition.

There beyond the pane to which he holds a light
must be mud or blood or fur draining in chaos;
a chthonic order just inconceivable,
one which might admit of mind carried

carefully down no few centuries unmired
by hands that bore their cold-suffered nights,
their hail-bitten days, herding, nutting, tired
to the bone of milking out a harder life than this.

'Grimpen' from 'Grimspound' from 'Grim'
from a mystery chalked up to the devil. Such a
struggle to believe in just a legacy of care
keeping family after family, keeping us, alive.

**TIRESIAS AT THE GALWAY INSTITUTE FOR
ENVIRONMENT, MARINE AND ENERGY**

They are setting a halter in the weight of the sea,
taking the measure of moon and storm
with the nerve and caution of precisely
uttered prayer. They are fossicking for grace
in the pull of a planetary mass: cylinders
blowing and gasping on the swell, cabled
through the dark into barnacled concrete below.
They are shucking the skin of an ocean,
leaving it to play across the panel-beaten west,
for this, a trickle of data, a current roping in,
pulse by pulse, across the sea-floor toward them.

Deference offered to the black water moving
beyond the wired glass, these heads bowed
over pencilled equations, over green ticking screens.
Until the good news comes: this is beginning
to work.   A blind man stands beside the water cooler,
whispers, 'Yes, this is good news indeed,' begins
to leave, to walk to Thebes to tell the king:
'Pay up, we need the real money now.'

THE HEAT
    Copenhagen, 2009

The land sealed over like cast bronze.
We skittered about like lizards
on a graveyard wall,
threw glances up at the silence
beating its horrible wings
over our heads.

And nothing from the judges
and nothing from the relatives
and nothing from the kings or their counsel.
Just this deep daylight blue panopticon
    getting quieter.

In the roar of traffic, silence.
In blaring wide-screen lounges, silence.
In frothing high streets Saturday afternoon, silence.
In the aviary banter of parliament, silence,
    an oven over the earth.

The whole island still as a desert night,
the clink and crack of it turning to glass
and all the bushes burning.

YEARS LATER

Prometheus is loading leisure centre vending machines.
Isotonic drinks, golden, foil-wrapped crisps, flapjacks,
chocolate *caramel-waferstoffeecrispychunkynutty* bars.
Turkish delight.　　　　He loves the smell of chlorine.
The flushed, breathless women in shorts, mothers-of-two
with freckles telling stories about their husbands. He loves
the strip lighting, the squeak of squash courts, the echoes
thrown through the sports hall like an aircraft hanger.
Everything managed just so. Coils of metal unspooling
enumerated confectionary.
　　　　　　　　　The thump
as it falls to the dispenser tray. The fact

that you can't reach an arm
up behind the glass
and help yourself.

A PARISH MAP
for Sylvia Kelly

She is ironing buttercup petals
and drying them under the carpet upstairs.

She is bringing them indoors by the armful
– embarrassed – from the hill up the lane at the back.

'*Golden* Hill': she has recently discovered
the gold is a landmark for migrating birds.

Imagine those dour carpets
fraying their edges, curled in one corner

and underneath, the skin of the sun itself
holding its tongue in the house's interior dark.

She is making a map, pressing
petal after petal onto paper, fixing them down:

an image of the hill that means so much to her
but where they are building a Tesco's now.

She shows her neighbours the map.
They will contribute their stories, memories.

Later she'll add what they tell her
in pen and ink. These small acts of caring

matter more than you might think.
They live in the earth beneath developments yet

like the skin of the sun holding its tongue,
like petals laid side by side in the busy dark,

patient, looking up
through the gaudy noise of the aisles above.

SKEW

The rain came flecking and pocking through bog-water rushes,
through the blackthorn scrub and the slopes of bilberry bushes.
It built in droves of flood-water slumping against the wind.

All day over the burnt-out ends of August's flowers,
ploughing its fingertips down through the soil. Rain,
strange rain, collapsed rain, hauled itself up

and collapsed again, drowning, scouring, filling those
mired valley sides, an intense consummation that
we soon felt we were intruding upon. Then it stopped.

Peat-beds gurgled. Light glinted in beads on the heather.
The air simply lifted around us – we never felt so heavy,
so grounded as then, bereft and exposed, in a brilliant wind.

There is no going back now, look at us standing speechless,
sun going down a red ultimatum and the drive home a journey
into a piercing, precarious moment where everything,
    everything matters.

HARBLEDOWN SOLSTICE

Now is the time of the long midwinter's ocean crossing.
Homes like tall boats go creaking through the dark.
Shouts sound, ropes drop; word goes round, we are off.
Children point out the moon on the water.
We cross in steaming kitchens, tilting and clinking.

Snow comes and buries the parish; snow
whose blank gravitas gazes west from Golden Hill.
Gusts buffet this day's small aperture of light.
"Hold Fast!" the shout goes up; the bells ring out
and we tip to the north through darkness again.

Do you remember, on the sloped raft of Duke's Meadow
we steadied ourselves and made out the Plough,
Orion, the Seven Sisters, and even the glowing cathedral
looked small below them? Here, bold swell of downs,
hold fast, go rising and falling above the city into the night.

HOME GROUND
for A. and G.

A hill knows more
than a pile of stones and soil.
It knows the lick of your before-birth dark
and keeps it in a forest of graves above you.
Slow hill, almost asleep hill, our hill together.
Flashing with frost and sun, ploughed, unploughed,
green with skidding, upturned winds.
Same hill, remaining hill, many-faced hill above us.

A hill knows less
than an angel but endures.
Its tawny shy eyes will roam
the underside of turf and tufted fields.
High, wise hill, horizon-scanning hill, patient hill,
with ears that hear the quake of coming futures
and read the booming depths of vaulted soil.
Hill among the crowded matter of the planet, deep hill, tall hill.

This one outstares the gargoyled night,
keeps the dark from burying us alive.
Anonymous, magnanimous, vanishing from time to time
among furniture, woods, rafters and stones.
Receding hill, underpinning hill, rumbling tummy of a hill.
Like a moon in a neighbourly orbit
weighing on the outer edge of mind and mood.
Calm hill, secret hill, kindly rampart written with paths and picnics.

MUFFLED

The oak copse drips with damp, slick black
against the heavy red dusk. These cold months
it knuckles into silence, tongues wound round
with rinds of bark and swallowed into lower,
weighty saps, nosing through the rootwork,
draining with a gurgle into flinted dark.

We stand, abandoned, in the clearing by the pond.
Not a soft thing shows against this closed
world, not the muttering hearts
of moles in hibernation, nor badgers,
buried, fogging their sett with stink.
Only the birds that in their toughness stayed,
straining through their body-fat with song
for the red earth pushing up toward the sun.

THAW

It is April outside the Santa Maria della Vittoria.
Those rays of plate-gold splayed over St. Teresa
begin to thaw. Gold into sunlight; sunlight into air,
air through the varnished wooden pews.

You can hear the traffic gusting from the streets.
It is like an ocean floor in here; dust motes
catch the light as plankton, but something
is changing, the woodwork is ticking awake.

Teresa, in the folds of her cloak, begins to breathe.
She does not look around her. She has not
been sleeping and knows exactly where she is.
She is holding a silence the size of an ocean about her.

She does not step down from her absurd pedestal,
walk out among the traffic, palms calmly
blessing the windscreens and horns of the city.
She has hardly opened her eyes.

She is listening to the starlings in the palm tree,
the sound of a straw broom on the marble and tiles.
A tear slides from the corner of an eye.
By the time it hits the floor, she is stone again.

SLOW LANDSCAPES
    Poems from the route of HS2

    I

    NEAR TWYFORD

The landscape   the landscape

         inside

    is a railway cutting
thirty feet deep in places and brimming with leaves,
a linear forest miles long all but hidden between slopes.

Down below the grazing and growing
it's a shadow of a place
where orange-lipped
fungi think deeply
and a small owl blinks
and shifts from foot to foot.

A kingdom of silver pools,
     refuge of subterranean grudges
         where things seem to come
to regroup, like the dropped conkers splitting their rinds,
to plot their countermeasures against the day.

Down here progress is difficult. Developments are
qualities of damp, rot, mulch in the blackening ground.
A hungry silence six or seven miles long grows fur
grows claws, growls like a wounded badger in the dark.

II

CUBBINGTON

Saint of the pear tree upstanding,
high one of the secret names,
two hundred or more years old
and ember-red this autumn
on a hill above the River Leam,
count us among those who were
good to you, before the diggers came.
Guardian of the cabbage fields,
watcher over Royal Leamington Spa,
shielder of picnics in high summer,
though you be split and uprooted,
though you be torn down now
at this late hour of your endurance,
remember us, who looked up
into your branches in all seasons.
High one of the secret names,
saint of the pear tree upstanding.

III

Ruins, Stoke Mandeville

A mound of headstones, churchstones,
bones, weeds and earth.
A circle of lime trees and railings around it.

Hollows in the meadow where fishponds
once were. 'This is not consecrated ground
but visitors are requested not to interfere.'

Two horses flirting over a gate nearby.
The setting sun like a dark idea
voices carefully through leaves.

You want to put an ear to the mound, find
a way down through these relics,
in and in to the terminus

where the dead will teach us
that leaving well alone
is its own kind of keeping;

those who are stopped but not vanished,
at rest among crockery and glass,
stars in a galaxy of soil.

THE CLIFF RAILWAY

There's a sliding of levers so greased beneath the carriage
you could be lifted by nothing at all. Maybe a thunk
in the gears and a baggy cable tightening, but otherwise
the ascent is heavenly, luminous, pulled sunward
through a granite canal by a counterweight of salt-water
dragged from the mouth of the Lyn. This is
Victorian engineering, lifting these two families,
and their solemn looking basset hound into the sky.

The sea slumps below us in a bowl, white light
cooking up a dream of a stranger and stranger sun;
the whole ascent also a backing away uphill. Iron rails
pinned and fixed in the earth, the spoked wheels,
double braking system, the speed and ingenuity,
all this capital investment cradling us up
from the edge of the sea; the dream is to keep going
spare no expense unto weightlessness, but here's

that swell in the knees as we come to a stop.
We file out, restored to the gravity we left
in a moment of well-oiled possibility
all over now. And we are finding our feet again,
not sure quite what just happened, quietly
milling about in the shadow of a flint-walled church,
two crows fighting over gravestones, an empty
bench looking past all horizons, and the naked air
                              suddenly chilling us to the bone.

HAWTHORN

We are three things against a winter sun:
a trunk strangled up from the earth and opened;
a globe of inward thorns; and roots
splayed through whatever soil is left on the chalk.

We will hang on to this near clod, strain
for the slower and slower ooze of sap.
We will hang on, bear down together
on this shallow-barked life-form.

Wet wood gurning apart into branches;
dividing and subdividing until there's nothing left to divide.
The stub-end of every thought
looking its limit in the face.

Beyond this bud or broken open leaf
or completely uttered berry –
an emptiness we do not know:
this glass too dark to see through.

When there is more bark to furrow
when there are more leaves to wring,
more knots to clench in consternation
we will furrow, wring and clench them.

We are going down below again
to stoke up the same old saps,
to wake up the ghost of the ghost
of the ghost in the gently sucking dark

BLOCKS
    Portland

                                    Huge
conciliated weights with brambles flowering over them.
      Serene, beatific stones, disinterested.
      Stones to unsettle a bad conscience.

A boy and a girl playing among them.
Count these ones. Look at this, come
to the edge, no, wait, go round it;
climb over, push here; no, try again,
lift from the legs; wait, stay where you are: Look up.

    Where will you find a place for this in your life?
    Something must be left.
    The sound of chisels a long way off;
    or are they near but muffled?
    It is a long way down, a long way up to the light.

        Here are your closed eyes, your bare skin,
        your paralysed thoughts swum out beyond their depth.
        Bright sun on the channel.
            Here is patience
            unfolded so many times there is only an outside left.

That chipped piece you've taken
in your pocket will weigh where you put it down at home,

press a dent on your desk and one day break the desk in two.

                          You will find hands
        and more hands closing around your ankles.
        I shine and you can hear in me
        the creak of ropes as thick as your arm.
        Rocks fall, they kick up dust and roll through the air.
        I will wake you in the night
        with the thought of these rocks falling.

The quarry wall, opened again and again,
weight beaming up from it, fissured, unclenching;
    calcite and sand grains in a tropical wash
    come to this, stilled,
    stalled, stopped,
    pressed for millennia
    ended, made,
    and won from the wall in blocks:
    now the shoving ocean everywhere is lifted from their backs.
        The relief of it makes them still.

ULTIMA THULE

> *'For who would ever have gone so near Heaven, and not ventured a little farther...?'*
> Daniel Defoe

At that cliff-edge plank of limestone they call
An Troigh Mhairbh, or 'the step that isn't there',

faintly, on a fine day, you can almost hear the shouts
of the long gone Phoenicians who just kept sailing north,

amazed as the days grew longer, thinking, perhaps,
their voyage blessed, this was the total light of the gods.

But at that fragile tongue of rock looking west
with the whole archipelago at your back, you'll ask

who among them first spoke up and suggested, hungry
and cold, that they should set a course for home.

ANNUNCIATION

The angel saw the architect
and said nothing;
and the architect stood before the angel
in silence.

So they remained
in this way for some time –
oak leaves fluttering in the wind,
crickets chirring across the hot meadow,

until finally the angel disappeared
and the architect stood there alone.

It was as if
the sky itself had receded
leaving only his open heart
glittering under the galaxy beyond.

And his hands, and his eyes
and his lungs
were empty
and the green meadow was suddenly greener
than the colour itself would allow

and he stood in the raw daylight
inexplicably afraid.

BIOGRAPHICAL NOTE

Jos SMITH was born in Canterbury, Kent in 1980. He lived in Liverpool and Nottingham for a time before settling in Devon where he works at the University of Exeter as a researcher. He is also the author of a critical study of the New Nature Writing and teaches and writes quite broadly on landscape and place in post-war British and Irish literature. He is currently working on a history of the arts and environmental charity Common Ground. Jos is also on the editorial panel of the online magazine *The Clearing*. His poetry, which has appeared in a range of UK magazines, pamphlets and anthologies, explores the imaginative possibilities of our relationship with landscape and place. He is a keen long-distance hiker and paid up member of The Cloud Appreciation Society.

Selected titles in Arc Publications'
POETRY FROM THE UK / IRELAND include:

D. M. BLACK
Claiming Kindred

JAMES BYRNE
Blood / Sugar
White Coins

DONALD ATKINSON
In Waterlight:
Poems New, Selected & Revised

JOANNA BOULTER
Twenty Four Preludes & Fugues on
Dmitri Shostakovich

TONY CURTIS
What Darkness Covers
The Well in the Rain
folk
Approximately in the Key of C

JULIA DARLING
Indelible, Miraculous
COLLECTED POEMS

LINDA FRANCE
You are Her
Reading the Flowers

KATHERINE GALLAGHER
Circus-Apprentice
Carnival Edge

CHRISSIE GITTINS
Armature

RICHARD GWYN
Sad Giraffe Café

GLYN HUGHES
A Year in the Bull-Box

MICHAEL HASLAM
The Music Laid Her Songs in Language
A Sinner Saved by Grace
A Cure for Woodness

MICHAEL HULSE
The Secret History
Half-Life

CHRISTOPHER JAMES
Farewell to the Earth

BRIAN JOHNSTONE
The Book of Belongings
Dry Stone Work

JOEL LANE
Trouble in the Heartland
The Autumn Myth

HERBERT LOMAS
The Vale of Todmorden
A Casual Knack of Living
COLLECTED POEMS

SOPHIE MAYER
(O)

PETE MORGAN
August Light

MICHAEL O'NEILL
Wheel
Gangs of Shadow

MARY O'DONNELL
The Ark Builders
Those April Fevers

IAN POPLE
An Occasional Lean-to
Saving Spaces

PAUL STUBBS
The Icon Maker
The End of the Trial of Man

LORNA THORPE
A Ghost in My House
Sweet Torture of Breathing

ROISIN TIERNEY
The Spanish-Italian Border

MICHELENE WANDOR
Musica Transalpina
Music of the Prophets
Natural Chemistry

JACKIE WILLS
Fever Tree
Commandments
Woman's Head as Jug